DISCOVER

The
Yorkshire Dales

John Potter

▲▲ **Gunnerside Meadows** Spring sunshine bathes the beautiful patchwork of fields, drystone walls and barns in this secluded valley close to Gunnerside in Upper Swaledale.

▲ **Aysgarth Falls** Just east of Aysgarth, these spectacular waterfalls are among Wensleydale's most popular attractions.

CONTENTS

MYRIAD

Arkengarthdale & Swaledale

Swaledale is at the heart of the northern Dales. Flowing through it is the river Swale, which rises high up on peat moors to the west in Cumbria. This area contains the upland villages of Keld and Muker, together with Gunnerside, Reeth and Richmond, the capital of Swaledale. Arkengarthdale is a tributary dale which joins Swaledale from the north-west, with Arkle Beck at its heart. It contains the tiny settlements of Arkle Town and Langthwaite.

▲▲ **Langthwaite** Walk over the packhorse bridge into this tiny village and you will feel yourself going back in time. The village and the Red Lion inn were used extensively in the filming of the television series *All Creatures Great and Small*. A track leads to Booze – a village with no pub!

▲▶ **Keld** This small village nestles snugly in the hills at the head of Swaledale. Its pretty stone cottages are clustered around a tiny square and the hamlet is the crossover point of the coast-to-coast and Pennine Way footpaths. A ten-minute stroll along the river Swale brings you to the dramatic East Gill Force, just north of the Pennine Way. Further along the river are two other waterfalls – Catrake Force and Kisdon Force.

◀ **Arkle** The tiny hamlet of Arkle Town is just south-east of Langthwaite, on the road to Reeth. From the village there is a fine view across the river to the escarpment.

SWALEDALE

Kisdon Hill The limestone mass of Kisdon Hill stands proud at the western head of Swaledale and there are many picturesque walks on and around this magnificent peak. This viewpoint is from Kisdon Hill looking south towards Muker.

▶ **Gunnerside** Surrounded by stunning windswept fells, this unspoiled picturesque settlement sits at the foot of Gunnerside Gill. The valley bottoms are dotted with attractive barns and drystone walls and, in early summer, the fields are carpeted with wildflowers.

▼ **Muker** The pretty village of Muker sits proudly above Straw Beck on a long ledge. The beautiful church of St Mary the Virgin is at the heart of the village and is famous for its colourful east window which depicts the scenery around the village, including the river Swale and Straw Beck. The traditional hay meadows which surround the village are breathtaking at any time of the year.

▲ **Reeth** Once a centre for knitting and leadmining, Reeth has a spacious, triangular village green from which there are stunning views of the surrounding Swaledale countryside.

▶ **Richmond** The capital of Swaledale is dominated by its huge and majestic castle keep, an amazing and well-preserved piece of 12th-century architecture. The town is among the most beautiful in England with many elegant Georgian houses, cobbled streets and pretty cottage gardens.

Wensleydale

This broad, fertile dale forms an arc cutting through the northern part of the region from east to west. At its heart is the river Ure which has a number of dramatic waterfalls such as those at West Burton and Aysgarth. The market town of Hawes is home to the famous Wensleydale cheese and to the Dales Countryside Museum. To the east a host of beautiful villages such as Castle Bolton, Leyburn and Middleham have marvellous attractions for the visitor.

▼ **Hardraw** This view of snow-covered fields and drystone walls near Hardraw was taken from a vantage point looking south towards Hawes where the Wensleydale creamery is located. The 96ft Hardraw Falls, the highest in England, are fed by both Fossdale Gill and Hearne Beck. The falls can only be reached safely by paying a small access fee and going through the Green Dragon Inn in the centre of the village – but the view is well worth the price!

◀▲ Hawes Known as the little capital of Upper Wensleydale, Hawes with its thriving farming community is Yorkshire's highest market town. The Hawes Livestock Auction Mart has weekly sales and is always well attended by both local people and visitors.

▼ Gayle A short distance north of Hawes, Gayle is a picturesque village at the foot of Sledale. The village has two old cotton mills on the banks of Duerley Beck. Gayle Mill, downstream from the main bridge, dates from 1776 and has almost all of its machinery in place.

▲ Duerley Beck The packhorse bridge is an ideal place to view the stepped waterfalls which cascade through Gayle.

7

ASKRIGG TO AYSGARTH

▲**Askrigg** The setting for *All Creatures Great and Small*. In the series the country vet's home was called Scaledale House; in real life it is Cringly House in the old marketplace. The skyline across the valley is dominated by Addlebrough.

▼**Bainbridge** This village in the heart of Wensleydale has a wide and sweeping village green with ancient stocks and mature hardwood trees overlooked from the east by the remains of an unexcavated Roman settlement. In the past, the great forest of Wensleydale dominated the area and the horn used to guide workers back home is kept in the Rose and Crown inn.

▲ **West Burton** This pretty unspoiled village is situated just south of Aysgarth at the northern end of Bishopdale. Nearby high fells rise steeply to form a spectacular setting. The annual May fair on the village green is guaranteed to draw crowds.

▶ **West Burton Falls** To the east of the village, and easily reached on foot, are the glorious West Burton Falls – a popular location for artists and photographers.

◀ **Aysgarth Falls** The attractive village of Aysgarth is best known for its spectacular waterfalls where the river Ure cascades down a series of limestone steps on the eastern fringe of the village. The three sets of falls are all within one mile of each other and are easily reached by a series of delightful riverside walks.

MIDDLEHAM TO CASTLE BOLTON

▲ **Castle Bolton** This small village, with its attractive green, is dominated by the massive fortress of Bolton Castle, visible for miles around and famous for its herb and walled gardens. In 1568 Mary Queen of Scots was imprisoned here for a year on the journey south to her trial and execution. More recently the castle was used as a location for the 1998 film *Elizabeth*. During the Civil War, Colonel Chaytor held the castle for the Royalist side until forced by starvation to surrender. The castle is open to the public and the dungeon and gardens are a favourite with visitors.

▲▶ **Middleham** The castle with its massive keep was built around 1170 and dominates the surrounding countryside between Wensleydale and Coverdale. It was once the home of Richard III. The town is linked to Leyburn by a cast-iron bridge. The surrounding countryside is a centre for racehorse training.

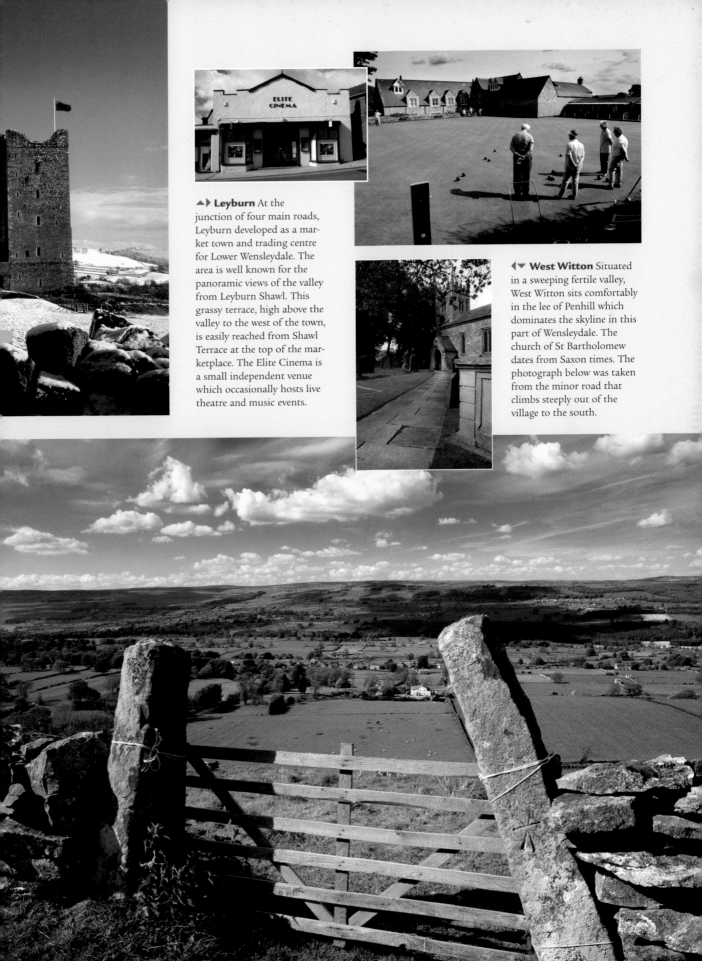

Leyburn At the junction of four main roads, Leyburn developed as a market town and trading centre for Lower Wensleydale. The area is well known for the panoramic views of the valley from Leyburn Shawl. This grassy terrace, high above the valley to the west of the town, is easily reached from Shawl Terrace at the top of the marketplace. The Elite Cinema is a small independent venue which occasionally hosts live theatre and music events.

West Witton Situated in a sweeping fertile valley, West Witton sits comfortably in the lee of Penhill which dominates the skyline in this part of Wensleydale. The church of St Bartholomew dates from Saxon times. The photograph below was taken from the minor road that climbs steeply out of the village to the south.

Dentdale & Ribblesdale

These two western Dales straddle the border with Cumbria giving this region its own distinct personality, ranging from lush green valleys to wild, windswept moorland. Dentdale (above) with its white-painted houses and softly rounded fells shares many characteristics with the Lake District. Ribblesdale, to the south, is at the heart of Three Peaks Country and has some of the most outstanding limestone scenery in Britain. Linking the area is the beautiful Settle to Carlisle railway line, one of the most scenic rail routes in Europe.

▲▶ Dent Situated close to two spectacular viaducts on the Settle to Carlise railway line, Dent station is the highest mainline station in Britain. Dent's many white-painted cottages are more Cumbrian in character than the mellow stone dwellings of the Dales.

▼ Brigflatts The Quaker Friends Meeting House at Brigflatts was built by the villagers in 1675. The village was then a self-sufficient community of around 75 people who ran their own cottage industries, relying principally on flax-weaving. In 1888 a raised wooden floor was fitted to allow water from the pond to flow through the meeting house without wetting the feet of the congregation.

▼▶ **Ingleton** This pretty market town is set amidst the unique and spectacular landscape of the limestone uplands of Ribblesdale, close to Ingleborough, one of the Three Peaks. Below ground this limestone region has dramatic underground rivers, caves and potholes which are a magnet for walkers and climbers. The narrow winding streets in the town centre are clustered around a tiny marketplace and nearby is the Victorian church of St Mary's which has one of the finest Norman founts in Yorkshire. The town is an ideal centre from which to visit the Ingleton waterfalls, White Scar Cave on Ingleborough (the longest show cave in Britain) and to view the grand viaducts of the Settle to Carlisle Railway.

◄ Ingleborough The unique and spectacular limestone uplands of the Dales contain three neighbouring peaks, Ingleborough, Pen-y-Ghent and Whernside, known as the Three Peaks. Ingleborough, the second highest, is pictured here from just below Runscar Hill shrouded in low cloud on a bitterly cold winter's day. The lower slopes have many caves and potholes including the cavernous Gaping Gill Pot on the western flank of the mountain.

▼ Kingsdale In the heart of Three Peaks limestone country are these two massive boulders, known as the Cheese Press Stones. They are a reminder of the time when cheese was pressed into shape between large stones when it was drying out.

▶ Ingleton Waterfalls A stone's throw from the village two rivers meet – the Twiss flows down Kingsdale and the Doe from Chapel-le-Dale. Both rivers cascade through a series of waterfalls and plunge pools. The largest and most famous, Thornton Force, is just a short walk from the car park in the village. Nearby White Scar cave brims with thousands of stalactites.

RIBBLESDALE

◀▲ Horton in Ribblesdale The start and finishing point of the famous Three Peaks Walk, Horton is also a popular stopping place for walkers tackling the Pennine Way. The local cafe provides much more than large pots of Yorkshire tea; it is also the place where Three Peaks' walkers clock in and out to register their progress on the walk. Each year there is a large entry of competitors in the famous Three Peaks fell race which takes place during the Horton Gala. The fastest runners will cover the 24-mile distance in just under three hours.

▶ Pen-y-Ghent Taken from the Pennine Way long-distance footpath on the remote Stainforth to Littondale road, this dramatic view of Pen-y-Ghent almost entices the walker to tackle this famous peak. The route of the Pennine Way follows this dead-end track for a short distance, then goes up and over the summit of Pen-y-Ghent, down to the village of Horton in Ribblesdale and then north to Hawes in Wensleydale. The lowest of the Three Peaks, Pen-y-Ghent's towering cliffs and escarpments more than make up for its lack of height.

▲▼ **Settle** This busy market town lies close to the Settle to Carlisle railway. The market square is surrounded by elegant Georgian houses, shops and courtyards. The Naked Man Cafe is popular with touring motorcyclists. A couple of miles from the town centre is the beautiful waterfall of Scalebar Force.

▲ **Ribblehead Viaduct** The 72-mile Settle to Carlisle railway line is one of the most picturesque in Britain and runs the length of Ribblesdale, with dramatic views of both Whernside and Pen-y-Ghent. This magnificent viaduct is just to the west of Ribblehead station. Built between 1870 and 1875 it is 104ft high, 1200ft long and has 24 arches.

Malham & Littondale

Malhamdale is famous for its limestone scenery, particularly Malham Cove – the 250ft high rockface which stands just behind the village. This dramatic scenery was created when massive slabs were forced to the surface during the last Ice Age. In some areas the effects of wind and rain have formed the limestone into large flat areas called pavements. A short distance to the north, Littondale is a lush green valley dotted with tiny hamlets and small farms.

▲ Malham pavement
Looking across Malhamdale from the limestone pavement at the top of the Cove. Close by is Malham Tarn, a large lake formed in the last Ice Age by glaciation. Nearby, Gordale Scar is an awe-inspiring gorge with magnificent limestone crags surrounded by high overhanging fells.

▼ Malham At the foot of the Cove the tiny village of Malham clusters around the stone bridge over the beck and the village green, with the Lister Arms on one side. The upper part of the village leads off towards Malham Cove and the road over towards Littondale. Malham has a youth hostel and a national park information centre, serving the needs of the walkers and climbers who gather to enjoy the area's unique scenery.

LITTONDALE

▲ **Foxup** There are four small settlements in Littondale – Arncliffe, Litton, Halton Gill and Foxup, which is the most remote. The hamlet is made up of a scattering of small cottages and farms, close to where Foxup Beck feeds the infant river Skirfare.

▶ **Arncliffe** The largest of the four villages, Arncliffe has a central open green surrounded by mellow stone cottages and farm buildings. Several large porched barns show that this is a typical Dales' working community. Arncliffe was the original setting for the television series *Emmerdale*. The church of St Oswald's lies close to the stone bridge over the river Skirfare. Depicted in the sidelights of the stained-glass east window are St Michael and St Oswald, the patron saints of Hubberholme and Arncliffe.

▶ **Hubbersholme** At the foot of Langstrothdale, this tiny hamlet is famous for the church of St Michael. Its choir stalls and pews are decorated with carvings by Robert Thompson, the "mouse man" of Kilburn, whose trademark "signature" is a small carved mouse which is found on all of his woodwork. Beyond the bridge, on the other side of the river, the cosy George Inn is a local favourite.

◀ **Halton Gill** The village of Halton Gill has a remote and beautiful location at the head of Littondale. Surrounded and sheltered by Horse Head Moor, Plover Hill and Cow Close Fell, the settlement stands proud just above the valley floor near to the infant river Skirfare. The 17th-century chapel in the village is combined with the schoolhouse. The village can be seen over the gate from the footpath to Foxup. Just above the two villages, at the confluence of the two streams which combine to make the Skirfare, is the lonely farmstead of Cosh House, said to be the most isolated dwelling in the Yorkshire Dales. This area has a strong link with those who fought the Scots at Flodden Field.

Wharfedale & Nidderdale

These two dales, located to the south of the region, run parallel to each other in a north-west to south-easterly direction. From Buckden down to Bolton Abbey, Wharfedale has magnificent upland scenery, including the massive bulk of Great Whernside, Buckden Pike and the stunning limestone slopes of Kilnsey Crag. Although it is one of the shortest of the main dales, Nidderdale has a great deal to interest the visitor including the settlements of Middlesmoor, Pateley Bridge and the beautiful Gouthwaite Reservoir.

▲ **Great Whernside**
This rugged hill dominates the skyline to the east of Buckden. Not to be confused with Whernside (one of the Three Peaks further to the west) it reaches a height of 2310ft and creates an abrupt change from the lush pastures in the valley below. The long boulder-strewn ridge gives extensive views across Nidderdale to the east and westward to Wharfedale.

◀▶ **Buckden** The annual Buckden Pike fell race draws runners from across the north of England, and watching the competitors aiming for the summit of Buckden Pike is a great spectacle. Close to the summit there is a memorial to the Polish crew of an aircraft that crashed here in 1942. There was just one survivor who managed to reach safety by following the tracks of a fox in the snow.

▶ **Kettlewell** Clustering around Cam Beck, close to its junction with the river Wharfe, this beautiful village has an annual scarecrow festival. These distinctive fields seen from a footpath just above Crookacre Wood lie south of the village.

▼ **Starbotton** The characterful grey stone cottages of Starbotton huddle around the Fox and Hounds inn, a popular retreat for visitors after walking along the riverside or exploring the nearby fells. This photograph was taken from the stony track that climbs out of the east side of the village.

WHARFEDALE

▲ Wharfedale in the snow
This view across Wharfedale
from Rowan
Tree Crag, looking towards
Hartlington Hall and Kail
Hill, was taken after a light
sprinkling of snow. Many
of the scenes in the film
Calendar Girls were filmed
in this part of Wharfedale.

▶ Kilnsey The tiny village of
Kilnsey nestles in the shadow
of Kilnsey Crag, a sheer wall
of limestone rising out of
the ground at the junction
where Upper Wharfedale and
Littondale merge. This
massive 170ft overhang is
a challenge much loved by
climbers and passers-by are
often seen gazing in awe
at their daring and agility.
The Kilnsey Show, one of the
largest agricultural shows in
the Dales, takes place each
August against the backdrop
of the Crag. The crags are
seen here across one of the
pretty fly fishing lakes which
belong to the Kilnsey Park
and Trout Farm.

Grassington The largest settlement in Upper Wharfedale, Grassington is centred on an attractive cobbled square where regular farmers' markets are held. At Christmas-time the shop-keepers dress in Dickensian costume and transform Grassington into a Victorian village; after dark, braziers are set up around the village square. On the Hebden road there is a national park information centre.

▲ **Linton** The stone cottages of this characterful village cluster around the village green which slopes down towards Linton Beck. Linton is a perfect village to explore on foot; the beautiful beck is crossed by a packhorse bridge, a road bridge and a "clapper" bridge – flat stones supported on piers.

APPLETREEWICK TO BURNSALL

▲ **Appletreewick** This peaceful Wharfedale village rests on a steep slope overlooked by the craggy summit of Simon's Seat. The main street is lined with stone cottages. The distinctive Mock Beggar Hall in the centre of the village was built on the site of a grange used by the monks of Bolton Abbey. It is rumoured that one wayward monk was walled up inside the hall.

▼ **Valley of Desolation** One of the most attractive and untouched areas of the Yorkshire Dales, this tributary valley branches off from Strid Wood towards the north-east. There are some picturesque waterfalls along the wood-land ravine which surrounds Posforth Gill. A delightful walk further up the valley leads to the rocky outcrop of Simon's Seat.

▲ **Strid Wood** Midway between Bolton Priory and Barden Tower this unique woodland is a Site of Special Scientific Interest because of its rare flora and lichen. The woodland was first opened to the public in 1810 by local rector William Carr who laid out forest paths, one of which leads down to the Strid, a narrow gorge on the river Wharfe.

▲ **Burnsall** Famous for the massive five-arched bridge which spans the Wharfe, the attractive village of Burnsall is seen here in winter from Rowan Tree Crag, shortly after sunrise. Every August the village hosts the Burnsall Feast Sports which include England's oldest fell race, when the bridge is decorated and thronged with spectators.

◀ **Bolton Priory** The ruined Augustinian monastery on the banks of the river Wharfe is a renowned beauty spot. Riverside walks wind through the woods to the gorge of the Strid. The beautiful village of Bolton Abbey, part of the estate of the Duke of Devonshire, can be reached on the Embsay and Bolton Abbey Steam Railway.

NIDDERDALE

▼ **Gouthwaite Reservoir** Looking down from Thrope
Plantation towards Gouthwaite Reservoir on the river Nidd,
a short distance above Pateley Bridge. Constructed in 1899,
the road which runs along the side of the reservoir gives access
to a nature reserve where there are birdwatching hides.

◀ **Middlesmoor** The stone cottages and cobbled streets of this ancient village huddle together at the top of the hill. From the graveyard of St Chad's church there are panoramic views down Nidderdale and across to the Hambleton Hills. In the distance, Gouthwaite Reservoir is just in view.

▲ **Pateley Bridge** The narrow main street is dominated by elegant, dark gritstone buildings. On either side there are pretty cobbled alleyways and passages which lead to hidden and quaint courtyards with a variety of cottages, galleries and craftshops. The town has England's oldest sweetshop.

Uredale

Once the river Ure leaves Wensleydale it continues along Uredale towards Ripon, passing the beautiful abbey at Jervaulx and the villages of Masham and West Tanfield. Less rugged than many of the more traditional upland Dales, Uredale is a prosperous and attractive farming area. The city of Ripon with its historic cathedral and amenities is an ideal centre for visits to the southern and eastern Dales.

▲▶▼ **West Tanfield** Situated on the banks of the river Ure, the skyline of this attractive village is dominated by the Marmion Tower and the medieval church of St Nicholas. The tower is a 15th-century gatehouse noted for its great arch and window. Sir John and Lady Elizabeth Marmion, who owned the tower, are commemorated in a tomb which can be seen in the church.

◀ **Ripon** The gateway to the eastern Dales, the cathedral at Ripon overlooks the riverside houses on the banks of the Ure. A church was first established here over 1,300 years ago; the present building is the fourth to have occupied the site. The town has three unusual museums – the Courthouse, the Prison and Police Museum and the Workhouse Museum.

▲ **Jervaulx Abbey** The beautiful ruins of Jervaulx Abbey lie between Masham and Leyburn. The abbey was founded in 1156 by Cistercian monks who moved from Fors, higher up the valley, in search of better weather. The abbey was ruined after the Dissolution of the Monasteries in 1537; much of its fine stonework was looted and used in other local buildings. Despite its condition, enough remains of the ivy-covered crumbling walls to remind the visitor of the simple yet austere lives of the "white monks". A delightful feature of this site today is the large number of wildflowers which decorate the ancient stones and surrounding parkland.

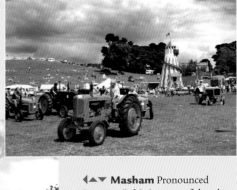

◀▲▼ **Masham** Pronounced "massum" this is a peaceful and attractive small town with a cobbled marketplace surrounded by elegant Georgian houses, stone cottages, shops and tearooms. The town is home to two famous breweries: Theakston and the independent Black Sheep Brewery. The Masham Steam Engine and Fair Organ Rally is a spectacular event which takes place every July.